Believing in the Planet

Believing in the Planet

Author: Myra Schneider

Published by Poetry Space Ltd 2024

Cover design: Martin Parker at silbercow.co.uk using a painting
by Robert Aldous, *San Vito lo Capo* (permission granted)

Poetry Space Ltd Company Number 7144469
Reg. Office: 2, North St, Beaminster, Dorset DT8 3DZ

Printed and bound in Great Britain by
Whitehall Printing, Bristol
www.poetryspace.co.uk
ISBN: 978-1-909404-55-7

Believing in the Planet
By

Myra Schneider

Myra Schneider

poetryspace

All profits from the sale of this book will be
divided between The Woodland Trust
and Dr Mark Sims' fund for Cancer Research UK
to be found at
justgiving.com/fundraising/mark-sims5

ONE

TWO

THREE

FOUR

ONE

Poseidon

After Robert Aldous: Poseidon

Never mind brilliant brains
and the theory of everything, plant yourself
on a seaweeded shore where wave after huge wave breaks

and white crests tower
into a sky which is boundless and packed
with angry clouds. Ocean will invade your head, drive

your thoughts away, pound
in your brain. You'll shrink from the black fury
swirling in these troubled waters and remember Poseidon rises up

whenever he sees a seal
with a car tyre round its neck, a turtle
struggling with a baby-blue mask, a cuttlefish with microplastics

lining its stomach. Worse
are the days he descends into the depths
and finds yet another coral reef drained of colour and deserted

by sea urchin, sponge and clam.
Enraged, he dives into the dark of a sea bed
deeper than Everest is high, roars orders at his waters till they attack

a town perched on a coast.
We weep to see buildings crumble, telegraph poles
topple and cars drown but still fail to appease the world's seas.

Pool

For Stephen and Marco

After David Hockney

The green thrum doesn't disturb the silence
as I push my way through damp grasses
between newly-leaved bushes to the pool

where the sun embraces my back as I stand
sniffing air untouched by traffic, longing to touch
the green pads bearing white petals poised like dancers

floating on the water's surface. Green is everywhere
and it glorifies the bushes by doubling them in water.
Crouching to watch water boatmen gliding over the surface,

I sense the busyness of beetles and worms wriggling
in the silty darkness below, think myself into it,
among larvae and hairy roots. Suddenly

I am stripping off smart phones and bombs, stripping off
presidents and fossil fuels, stripping off cars and envy,
love and poverty, stripping off logic, speech,

skin and bone, thinking how my origins, all origins
go back four billion years to the dark depths
of the sea where single-celled microbes,

next-to-nothings, first inhabited this planet.
Why is it, I wonder, that thoughts and ideas
always begin in a dark which can't be measured?

And I feel the inexplicable power of creativity
pulsing through this pool even though
it's a watercolour sketch on a page in a book.

Grass

No way to block the noise of the unwieldy machine
that's racketing along the pavement and drowning the whirr
of passing traffic as it crops the grassy verges.

I trail along the stark street, stare at a solitary
yellow-gold dandelion that's somehow evaded the chop,
at mindlessly uprooted clover plants, crushed daisies,

limp petals of a roadside poppy and tell myself
the grass will rise again but wonder when. A clump
of unmutilated dock leaves offers no consolation,

nor does the breeze which fails to ease the humidity.
I pause by a frontage near ours, breathe in
the scent of green needles from its thriving pine trees.

If only this mini-wood could cancel the heat
thrown up by the sheets of concrete now planted
instead of flower beds in most front gardens along our road.

*

This morning after a night of listening to rain pattering
on my window, I throw open the back door and step outside
to sniff the air's sweetness. Bluetits and goldfinches

are fluttering in and out of the plum trees as if to celebrate.
Beyond the lawn the elderberry and bramble bushes
merge into the soft layers of the park and I think of him: Hockney

in his garden in Normandy and all the months he spent
studying the character of every tree, the different weathers,
the patterns slow and fast rain make on the surface of his pool.

Once again, I open his book and remember how the green
of the unfettered grass, the trees coming into blossom
nurtured me as I struggled back from illness two autumns ago.

Horsetails

For Jennifer and Den

Horse pipes, scouring grass, snake grass –
puzzle grass, the names are so suggestive
they dance through my imagination. The thought

of this grass as a horse's tail makes me smile
and I'm amazed to find out it's distantly related
to the first plants and trees which grew on our planet

many millions of years before dinosaurs existed.
I stop reading and go downstairs to make supper,
remember a hot summer day of trailing for hours,

body aching, by a river banked with masses
of horsetails. I picture their long stalks jointed
like flamingo legs, try to picture the ancient planet.

Later, as I'm undressing for bed, darkness blots out
everything and the air begins to whirr as though
it's a giant fan. Giddy, I close my eyes,

certain this isn't a power cut. When I open them,
after minutes, hours, months, maybe years,
I'm gazing at trees whose tall, rough trunks

are topped with ferny growths and all around me
are scatterings of smaller plants, some fernlike,
some with horsetail seed-heads. The ground

is parched but I'm by a large pool or maybe a river
and not far away a waterfall is tumbling down
a crag. It's warm and the air is heavy, desiccated,

yet it smells of damp. The silence is palpable,
alien. I tug at a horsetail until a piece of stalk
comes away. Something moves by my toes –

a creature with a fat fishlike body and flippers
like feet. It scuttles into the pool and disappears
but while I'm searching for more of these creatures

the daylight drains away and I'm stranded
in the dark. Slowly, I see I'm staring at the carpet
in my bedroom. Confused, I go to the window.

The moon's emerging from the rucked linen of clouds
and I make out the eerie shapes of our plum trees,
the thicket in the park and the arches of the viaduct

by the stream. The stalk I picked has vanished
but the scuttling fish, the thin ferny trees are still
in my head – I must have travelled back aeons.

All those millennia life has been blossoming
on the planet. Turning away from the window,
I try to block out what we're on the brink of losing.

Hardwicke's Woolly Bat

On nights when the world's weathers snarl
how sweet to lie in bed and picture
the tousled body smaller than your little finger,
its tiny triangle ears, bead eyes

and the beautiful leaves of its upraised wings
which fold tidily away to allow it to slip
into a green pitcher's flaunted cup.
Surprising but neat, the life-style of this plant

which inhabits swampy forest floors: it's a lodging
at night in return for the visitor's droppings
which provide its host with breakfast. It comforts you:
the bat's snug fit in the pitcher's chamber,

the utter peacefulness of a sleeping creature
who knows it's hidden from predators.
Where can we curl up and sleep safe from fear
in this world we're continually wounding?

An Elephant

has taken up residence on my doormat,
no ordinary elephant. When the hall dims
how his body, patterned in gold, shines.
I whisper to myself he's a moonchild.

A flower stems from his uncurling trunk,
another blooms from the leaflike lobe
of his ear. His eyes are a series of rings.
On his ceremonial coat: semi-circles,

suns and stars sing, bracelets decorate
his legs. He brings festival to my house.
Elephant, you who remember everything,
hold birth parties, swaddle your newborn

with motherlove, take care of the sick
in your tribe, rage when you're upset, mourn
your dead with funerals, cover their bodies
with grass, weep silently, I welcome you.

In the pit of night when chill and anxiety rove
you wrap me in warmth, lull me with a sense
of security even though we both know
no one, nothing is safe in this life.

Walking with Francesca

For Francesca

I'm walking down our road with Francesca on a morning
when the sun is in bloom, when dandelions are bursting
into yellow and blossom is singing on the slender branches

of the prunus trees which beautify the verges. Francesca
waves to our friendly postman. In a few days she's going
for a month to Ghana. I picture her eating mangoes

fresh from a tree, cutting juicy slices from pineapples
and buying a basket of tomatoes at a market.
'Your walking is amazing', she says when I make

my neatest turnaround yet to position myself to walk back
home. For moments the midday sun is so warm it feels
like July – maybe by then we'll make it to the park, watch dogs

rolling around in ecstasy on the grass. She tells me
about Ghana's wildlife – the parks with jaguars, bison
and giraffes. And there they are: the giraffes, necks jutting

above the traffic as they search the streetlights for foliage
to munch. Beyond them a covey of elephants is trampling
the grassy roundabout at the end of the road, trunks

curled round the bushes and birch trees, ripping them
out of the ground. And I laugh as they revel in their feast
while four packs of vehicles snorting in fury grind to a halt.

Jungle

For Maika

It's January but outside the lawns and grassy verges
are very green after months of rain and the palm trees
in the frontage at the end of our road are thriving.

I love the spread fans of their spiky leaves
and the yellowish cacti spears underneath them –
they jump me to a holiday we had years ago

in Trinidad where our bodies always felt clammy
and even the grass smelt of heat. A mini forest
is flourishing next door and every year the amount

it's grown surprises me. On the verge
dandelions are in flower and I wonder if the planet
is forgetting winter cold. The parakeets have disappeared

from our back garden but they'll be back by spring
and maybe screeching cockatoos will arrive too.
Last night I dreamt I heard tomato frogs

croaking in the brook at the bottom of our park
and I smiled at monkeys swinging on our plum trees,
believing England had reverted to rainforest.

Planting

November, and without leaving the house,
without trowelling into finely tilled soil,
without lifting a watering can,

simply by pressing keys on the computer
I plant an avocado tree in Kenya.
How powerful, how useful I feel.

December, and in the pit of night I dream
a cord passing under the ocean is linking me
with the embryo tree because I'm its mother.

In January I read that storm clouds of locusts
are eating their way through East Africa,
picture the invaders devouring my plantlet

and stare at images of Kenya shorn of vegetation.
This is not like the plague God caused
long ago in order to punish Egypt's pharaoh,

this is entirely our doing. Utterly empty,
I press keys to send money for the hungry,
stand at the window staring at winter's greys.

Still grieving in sun-drenched April,
I plant a fig tree in the garden and will it
to grow, to open hundreds of green fingers

and bring forth hard buds which will swell
into soft purple pouches crammed
with sweet flesh, hordes of seeds.

The Glory

The almost dazing yellow of a huge dandelion head
on the grass verge, stops me in my tracks.
I stoop to examine its florets – they're mango orange
near the receptacle at the centre where a honey bee
has settled down to stuff itself silly on nectar.

Nothing humans invent can compare with this plant's
astonishing complexity, the loveliness of its transparent
blow-away globe holding seeds which the wind will scatter.
Oh my, now I see that dandelions are bursting out
all over: on the edges of concrete hills that run

from gateways to garages, in gaps by walls and on patches
of earth no one has stifled. I gaze at some that are vying
with bluebells and celandines. Clumps of tulips are busy
conferring and I love it that plenty of trees thrive here
in spite of the dawn to long-after-dusk rush of cars.

In this frontage, firs and pines have become a mini wood.
A few doors down a palm is showing off fans of fronds
as if it's an elegant dancer, and along the verges
prunus trees are crammed with dreamy pink blossom.
Our road is in its glory and I'm jubilant for the rest of the day.

But when I go to bed and close my eyes what I see is tarmac
riddled with potholes, broken concrete and dried-out mud
in front gardens, houses with gaping holes in once-windows,
roofs that have fallen in, heaps of rubble. There's not
a plant to be seen. Suddenly there's a gust of wind

which stinks of burning metal and now I'm too hot and facing
a wall of fire. It's higher than the one telegraph pole
still standing and advancing fast. Clouds of black smoke
are billowing overhead, swallowing the last patches
of blue sky. The heat's unbearable. Terrified, I turn,

try to run but roaring flames surround me. Unable to breathe,
I start choking but at last I force my eyes open, clutch
at the softness of the mattress beneath me, grope for the lamp
on the shelf, with a trembling hand pick up a glass of water.
Gulping the cool liquid, I picture dandelions and weep.

Longing for Rain

For Ruth S

I hurry outside hoping for fresh air but the smell
of grit makes me cough. Far down the road
I can see a huge truck churning up specks of tar

and two doors away a drill is breaking up the frontage –
now it will always be flowerless. I think of our lawn,
pale, thirsting for rain for weeks but none is forecast.

Yet as I stare at the pavement, I'm stunned to see
tiny-leaved stitchwort growing in the cracks
between broken slabs where tree roots are trying

to break through and maybe it's the heat this August
which has brought out the packs of ants. I love
the determination to survive. On the over-dry verges

clovers are growing and in one garden I glimpse
the emerald gleam of bluebottles' backs. And bees,
every kind of bee: bumbles, honeybees, masonry bees

and wasps as well as insects I don't recognise,
are buzzing round golden rod and the spiked heads
of alliums which, when they're dead, look like tiny planets.

Arid

Such an ugly word! It conjures up scrubland,
scabby-leaved thorn bushes, straggles
of grey grass, unsightly patches of bare earth
somehow reminiscent of heads losing their hair.
It conjures up rubbish dumps where nothing
but rats and bugs thrive among forlorn
bicycle wheels, shoes bereft of their partners,
mashed tins that once housed hearty soups.
It suggests a gravelly voice, a cheese grater's face,
boredom, empty cupboards, empty minds.

Now, open your book and look at a day of rain –
rain falling in long determined strokes on grass,
tree and hill. No aridity here, no drought,
no wildfires. Let the wet air cleanse your lungs
as it seeps through grass into the earth, feeds
slithering worms and crowds of millipedes and ants
making their way among roots and stones.
Let it loosen the dry cough in your throat,
quieten all your nagging uncertainties,
lullaby your senses. Receive it as a blessing.

Fishing Boats

For John F after Derain: Le Séchage de Voiles

I refuse to inhabit today so I've taken myself
into the silence of my study and now I'm slipping back
to 1905 in Collioure. Here I am, young again

and limber, walking round the harbour bay
to the fishing boats lined up at the top of the beach.
Their white sails are hoisted to dry and, though a few

are sprawling, the rest are taller than the red-
roofed buildings standing behind them. Their tips
touch humps of flamingo-pink and lavender hills.

A breeze is tickling the sea which loves the sails
so much it grabs their reflections, stretches them out,
melts their whiteness into its cobalt. I'm revelling

in the robust air and everywhere it's out and about:
that child in a red dress, the sailor striding past
in his blue uniform, an elderly couple, both

dressed in white, ensconced in a rowing boat
that's dawdling its way through the water. The door
to a café is open and I catch the tinny sound

of someone thumping out a tune on a piano
but as I near the fishing boats the din the wind
makes as it slaps sails and shakes rigging

drowns every other sound. I think of Derain
in a fever of excitement that long sunstruck summer
as he sat painting huddles of lime green,

ripe yellow and ultramarine hulls standing
on hot orange sand or bobbing at the sea's edge.
A jolt and Collioure disappears. Bereft, I drift

into my bedroom, smile at the pink flowers
patterning the deep purple cover on my bed,
at the fistfuls of green dotting every tree outside.

Wild

I can't believe it: the garden mindlessly shorn,
the buddleia bush, its tousle of honey-scented
purple cones with myriads of orange-dotted,
nectar-packed florets adored by butterflies,
no longer spilling over the steps descending
to the garden, the plum trees lopped unlovingly,
fruits tumbled and crushed underfoot, the lawn –

true it was a raggle-taggle meadow – now
it's hairless! Every shrub has been beheaded,
weeds removed by giant electric tweezers
which droned all morning but the soil, the dear
dried-out soil in need of digging over,
lies untended by spade and fork – maybe
they've been dismissed as tools of a bygone age.

Yes, it's spick and span out there like a room
where visitors worry about dropping cake crumbs,
a room that's weighty with knick-knacks,
cushions, the absence of tenderness and books –
but I don't want to tread on grass with the texture
of a Persian carpet that's been over-hoovered.
Banish severe and finickity, banish spray polish!

What I want is wild: our pushy, self-planted
raspberry canes tangled with a bush whose currants
gleam like gems of the imagination. I rush
to the park, gorge on its green freedom, its stream
slovenly with long-haired weeds and trailing stems,
its mud island where my child used to play,
the cool of trees healing the car-polluted air.

Birds

Half-dressed, I plant myself by the bay windows,
raise my arms above my head, and slowly lift
the weighty grey sky. Then, with a sword in each hand,

I stretch my arms out to left and right – that's when I notice
the geese, a V of them, necks stretched forward,
flying northwards high above the park's sycamores.

A minute later I glimpse them flying back again
to whatever pool they came from. By then I'm trying
to brighten the day by pulling on a cherry-red sweater.

A few magpies smartly attired in black and white
are strutting about on our raggedy lawn as if they owned it
and some pigeons are up by the fence busily pecking

at the ground. They take off though as a mob of parakeets
swoop down and lay siege to every tree I can see,
every bush. Squawking, the invaders snap up grubs

and the odd rotten apple. Two of them even hang
upside down by their claws on a dead sunflower head.
They look like lime-green leaves shaking in the breeze

as they quarrel over the few seeds still left among
the limp petals. When they rush off, the sunless garden
seems to be laden with hopelessness but later

I spot a blackbird alighting on a branch that's still sporting
some leaves. The sun comes out as its yellow beak opens.
How it gladdens me that birds still believe in the world.

The exercises described in the first two verses are movements in the
ancient Chinese practice of qigong.

Taormina

For Ruth G

I peer out of the kitchen window at the November fog
trying to push its chill indoors, then rummage in the past
until I almost believe I'm there on that rocky peninsula,

sunlight warming my body as I gaze at the glorious azure,
turquoise and lapis lazuli of the sea below the cliff
and the arm of the coast stretching into the distance.

Soon I'm conjuring up the old town that clings to a steep hill,
the lemon trees on its narrow pavements, its shops crammed
with patterned plates and bowls, the scarlet geraniums

in window boxes on the balconies and sills of cramped cafés
I can even smell the wood-fired stoves in busy pizzerias.
And I remember the afternoon we scrambled high up

above the town, grasping at stones among tufts of thyme
and oregano – bees were sucking nectar from tiny flowers.
Perched there we could see droves of people below

in holiday sunhats and trainers buying tat from stalls
in the narrow road leading to the theatre the Greeks
hacked out of the cliff twenty-seven centuries ago.

In the far distance was Etna's thin plume. And now
it comes back: the evening the volcano erupted: clouds
of smoke billowing, gold and red fire mingling and competing

with the scarlet of the setting sun. The image stays,
reminds me how small we are in this astonishing world,
how grievous it is that we don't act to save it.

TWO

Flame

After Chris Holley, Flamenco Shawl series, mixed media on paper

It's the darkest of darks, the pit of the year
yet from a cavern that must be studded with light
in the far below that's as black as night,

she rises. You gasp when she opens a shawl
feathered with flames, swirls and swirls it
across the sky, wonder if she's slipped out

of a dream. She seems to be weightless
and your heart thumps, afraid she'll blow away
before you sup to the full on her brightness.

But look at her supple body – how sturdy
it is and as her back arches to dance you see
knee muscle and ankle beneath her gown.

Now, she's queening the huge star-laden sky,
calming the distress planted within you
when you were a child in the long ago.

Now, she's soothing the fears which howl disaster
as they circle this world. *Who is this creature*?
you ask and the reply comes: *your inner fire,*
nourish her or she will be extinguished.

The Water-Tree

Hokusai: The Kirifuri Waterfall at Mt. Kurokami in Shimotsuke Province

It halts me in my tracks just as it's halted
the three pilgrims tiny at its foot
and as I stare at the bunches of thin branches
worming their way through the foliage
clothing the mountain, then plunging
with a force neither man nor machine
could deflect,
                        I suddenly see they're roots
spreading out fingers to claw
at the river rampaging far below
and dig into its silty bed. The world
of everyday, our terrible mistakes
slide off
                        and although I'm fettered
in my study three centuries
and thousands of miles away, self
disappears into the water-tree's triumphant
white roar, into the packs of green bushes
clinging to those steep slopes, eager
to worship the everywhere water.

Honey

For Simon

When the light is small at the end of the year
and you've forced yourself outside,
been bitten by a wind from the east,
be glad that you're lucky enough
to own a warm house you can retreat to.
Once inside you will forget
that mean December is pulling down
night, shut out the sense
that everything is declining. Go
into the kitchen and look again
at the jar of clear honey you put
on the white counter this morning
when the sun was briefly out.
Then, you saw in its glass tiny, immaculate,
an image of the trees in the park,
a dazzle-dot of light beside them,
and fainter, elongated, a section of yourself
in your long-sleeved pink top.
Now, you note the amber of the honey
seems darker but the jar has enticed
the light from the ceiling to flow down
one of its sides. You try to catch
an image of your face but it refuses.
For a few moments you feel unreal,
as unreal as the glimpse you suddenly
have of yourself aged four, eating bread
spread with margarine and liquid gold
at an enamel-topped kitchen table.
Put the jar down and, thinking of bees
on your lavender bushes in summer,
warm a crumpet under the grill,
spread it lavishly with butter and honey,

kick your fears for yourself, your nearly
birdless garden, the whole world,
under the table and for a few minutes,
sink your teeth into cushiony sweetness.

Brussel Sprouts

For John K

When the February sky is weighty with clouds and the wind,
a ferocious animal, knocks over fences and rickety sheds,
rushes rubbish down streets, rocks trees madly,
tears off their branches and crashes them to the ground,

when the paper is packed with such grim news
you throw it in the bin, take a bagful of Brussel sprouts,
those small globes which grow on knotty stalks
topped with floppy leaves. You will be surprised

to discover these hardy winter characters
are axillary buds from which long stems would sprout
and yellow flowers bloom if they're left in the ground.
Pick one up, hold it between thumb and index finger,

sniff its freshness, touch its skin and consider
its construction which is more subtle than any work of art.
Feel the density of its layers – they fit together more tightly
than the dressing gown and duvet you pull round your body

as you lie in bed in winter trying to fend off reality
by conjuring up the summer sun's dazzling gold. Simmer
these small vegetables for a few minutes, then sit down
to savour the warmth of these small green balls.

Gold

For Ben and Luciene, my son and daughter-in-law.
After Robert Aldous, San Vito lo Capo

It's the gold of that rocky peninsula in Sicily,
a gold more potent than the red of Caribbean sunsets,
a gold that mocks the amber of the rich liquid
pressed from olives and hoarded in pitchers in cellars.
It outdoes the dark shine of woodland honey,
belittles the soft yellow of eucalyptus honey.

It's the moment that blazing gold mass meets
the sea and dissolves in its cornflower blue water
which slowly becomes violet, cobalt and at last
lapis lazuli. It's the sea seeping into the Madonna blue
of a sky that dissipates the purple clouds disgorged
by Mount Etna and sifts into clouds of unknowing.

First Night of the Proms

1

The untidy sitting room slips off our shoulders
and as it folds away we discover we're in the Albert Hall.
The air is taut, we are taut. We are mesmerized

by the face of the conductor who is weaving together
the sounds of many instruments,
bringing the singers to life, drawing them

into the tapestry. Somehow, we are part of this
and somewhere I sense Vaughan Williams.
He is leading us through the nooks, dells and pools

of Shakespeare's dream islands. The music falls away
into silence. A timeless gap, then the audience
comes to life, fills the air with applause.

2

Now we are in a world of electric reds, luminous golds,
marine blues and great volumes of sound led
by the organ which is as majestic as the prow of a ship.

All eyes are on the player who pulls out stops
and commands two rows of keyboards and pedals.
A mirror connects him with the orchestra

and their passionate conductor who's almost floating
in her gown. A glinting army of pipes assaults the screen
and the whole world it seems, only exists inside the music

even when it sinks to almost nothing
before rising up again and again in massive waves
until finally it retreats into the huge silence of the audience.

The Jazz Concert

After Chris Holley, The Jazz Players

The smell of summer warmth taut
with expectancy is rising from the grass
and there they are: four musicians
playing on guitars, drum and percussion
to a Saturday crowd who have kicked off
the dull of everyday. Some are lounging
on the grass with their kids who are licking
fast-melting ice cream cones,
some nod to the beat, some click fingers
and suddenly you discover you too
have stripped off the mundane,
you too are sitting on the daisied,
sun-drenched grass with music
throbbing through your body. Now
the drumming grows louder,
the rhythm quickens, becomes
the excitement of fast cars
belting through a night-time city
whose shop windows are lit up to entice.
And everything is heat and colour:
the strident red of the musicians' jackets,
the marine blue of the two guitars,
the corn yellow thrown by the sun.
And as the fast becomes even faster
you throw out all the worries
which weigh heavy on your mind.
Happiness wells up inside you
and even when the playing stops
and the instruments are laid down
you feel as grand as a Steinway piano
and the electrifying music
goes on playing in your head.

Lotus Leaves Swaying in the Breeze

In memory of Paul Flavell, qigong teacher

Find a place where silence strokes your body
and quietens your mind, then point your thumbs
towards your back and touch your hips lightly

with your fingertips. Breathe in as you let your arms
rise slowly to chest height and relish the strength
of your stem – it's rooted in lifegiving silt.

Now turn your hands over and as your leaf-
laden arms are gently blown forwards
let go of your breath. Allow the playful wind

to blow the leaves outwards as far as they can go.
Relax as they move together again – and it's now
as they sway towards your heart that you see him –

his central stem is the trunk of a slender lotus tree.
He has planted it carefully on the carpeted floor,
discarded his crutches. He steadies himself,

one leg at a time and as he slowly opens his arms
you see you're in a forest of lotus leaves swaying
in the breeze. His eyes miss nothing, he knows
the ins and outs of everyone in the silent room.

Lotus leaves swaying in the breeze is an exercise in the ancient Chinese practice of Qigong

The Word

For Justina

What luck to lay hands on it on a morning
when the sky is in deep sulk, when leaves are dying
in helpless thousands and the grief-stricken planet
is losing its battle against the disease of rubbish.

I grab it with relief, proclaim it to the unhoovered room:
manifold – the three satisfying syllables seem
to gleam, to be imbued with a warmth, an optimism
which kickstarts my sorry-for-itself mind.

Manifold: a word as purposeful as the newly
risen moon, a word with its feet firmly
fixed on the ground as it spurs me to search it out
in the Oxford English Dictionary on the internet.

Evading cookies, I discover the origin is neither
man nor *field*. Centuries old, it's tethered
to the Anglo-Saxon *manigfeald*, has more character
than *abundant*, *varied*. At once I'm hurtled back

to that rugged age, to the story of Beowulf, who fought
monstrous Grendel in the mead hall one night
after the sun's candle was snuffed, to Caedmon,
a tongue-tied cowherd, who found words when told

in a dream to write about the making of the world.
And look, I'm now standing waist-high in a meadow
freckled with poppy reds and buttercup yellows –
and manifold has become a million-petalled flower.

Million-petalled flower: Philip Larkin

The Persian Robe

After Matisse, The Persian Robe

You wonder what she's thinking as she sits leaning
her elbow on the balcony table by a sea-green vase
and a scattering of red and orange-cheeked apples.

You envy her pantaloons which are also sea-green
and her purple robe which reaches to the floor –
everything suggests she hasn't a care in the world.

Suddenly, you want to be there, are on tenterhooks
to escape from your house as if it's become a prison.
The garden and park beyond it pall too even though

you love watching leaves yellowing on the trees
and your heart skips on mornings when mist rises
from damp grass as pale light breaks through cloud.

You would sit down at her table below those
large-lobed fig leaves, breathe in warmth,
the scent of salt and thyme in the breeze and forget

that the world you live in is riddled with disease,
plagued by drought and flood. Relaxing in silk
on her balcony above the beach, you'd gaze

at a pitcher which might have stored olive oil
in the cellar of a palace in ancient Crete, laze
the day away as she is free to do… But it's 1940,

Europe is at war. Here in Nice, people are safe
for the moment but she might have family in the Nazi-
occupied north, or a lover who's a soldier

and has been reported missing, is maybe dead.
Sitting here, perhaps she can forget war for a while,
feed on the quiet of apples, the blue of sea.

The Three Trees

For Sheila, my sister.
After Paul Nash: The Three

Leaning so closely together their heads touch,
they rise into a pale sky where birds are wheeling.
With their spindly bodies and faces shaped

like strange kites they make me think
of the many underfed and I see them as friends
striving to support one another. Looming

above a tiny cottage behind a hedgerow,
they cast eerie shadows on the stubble field below.
Is it their isolation which reminds me that as far back

as I can remember I longed for trees? None grew
near the house above the Clyde where I spent
my 1940s childhood, none in the nearby fields

edged with brambly hedges, none on the moor
whose sandy paths we often scrambled up,
not minding the rough heather which scratched our legs.

On the ridge at the top there were stretches of bog
with white wind-blown flowers. Above, curlews cried
and in the distance, oh joy, stood the fir woods

where we sometimes picnicked with mother.
Here, my sister and I revelled in the dense darkness
beneath branches, searched for signs of magic.

I look again at the lonely three on the card,
remember Sussex, where I lived in my teens,
and the Downs where trees abound, re-live

climbing up the chalky path that took me to Stoke Clump,
a ring of beeches rising against the skyline,
a place where I felt safe from the angers

always threatening to explode at home. The three
offer no haven. I stare at them struggling
upwards as if trying to escape from our planet.

Turkey Tails

Whenever I come across a strutting turkey
in an advert or on the internet, fear jumps up,
jams my throat and, before I can stop it,

rushes me back to the childhood day
my father walked us for miles over moors
and across fields hedged with brambles. We halted

at the five-barred gate of a farmyard we needed
to cross and I stared, not at puddled mud
and dung, but at the turkeys – two of them,

the raised fans of their tail feathers and worse,
the huge red bulges on their beaks
and gobbling throats. Terror clamped my body.

I was sure those vicious beaks would peck my flesh
and the sickening masses of feathers would engulf me
if I dared to take a single step beyond the gate.

Even my father's furious 'stop being so stupid'
failed to make me move my clammy body.
Did I manage to bypass the yard by squeezing

through a prickly hedge or did my mother, trying
to shush my screams, guide me past the birds
who smelt my fear and advanced, flapping wings?

My days of walking in fields and avoiding farmyards
are long past but when I came upon the image
of turkey tail mushrooms in a book this morning

fear sickened me for a few moments
but then I was seduced by the row upon row
of frilled fans with blueish and brown ribbings.

I knew too that I'd seen this fungus on a tree stump
and assumed it was packed with poison but now
I've found out it can heal and I'm filled with wonder.

The Conical Shell and the Bladderwrack

For Mark R. After Annie Soudain

The conical shell and the bladderwrack
remind me how much I miss the seashores
of my childhood: Inellan where the sand
was ribbed by the waves, Arran's sandy beaches,
unprinted by other feet, which seemed to stretch
into ever, the roughness of the wind salted
by the sea – they were my idea of paradise.
The beach at Gourock, where I lived as a child
during World War Two, was spoilt by tar
washed in by the tide. We played above the tideline,
pulled the turreted shells of whelks off bone-dry rocks,
stared at the soft tubular beings within,
made our fingers bleed trying to prise off limpets,
not knowing that when the tide went out
some slipped from their granite perches
and were washed out by the sea
which refreshed their jellied bodies.

Sometimes we cracked the bladderwrack pods
but I've never seen the plant in flower
as it is in this painting. The white cliffs
in the distance remind me of the day
we left the long promenade by the sea
at Eastbourne where I was recuperating
from months of hospital treatment. I was frail
but triumphant the ordeal was over
and each step I took as we climbed up high –
higher than the pier standing on thin
birdlike legs, was a kind of victory, a refusal
to give in to my ageing body. At last, we reached
the grassy plateau, stood at the viewing point.
I stared at the sheer drop and the white-crested waves.

Exultant, I didn't ponder about the sheer cliff
formed by shells which once held tiny
soft-bodied creatures. I was in my glory.

Gannets

At the kitchen window I'm watching the wind
force every tree in sight
to dance crazily when the radio cuts in
with warnings about storm-driven waves
flooding seaside towns. Turning,
I glance at a picture of gannets pinned
on the noticeboard. Struck by the size
of their wingspan
                    I hurry upstairs and, ignoring
a tart voice in my head which points out
that my decades-old body is not fit to climb
to the top of a cliff and watch birds
in flight, I sit down at the computer,
click on 'you tube'.
                    At once my small room
vanishes and there they are: gannets high
in the sky. Mesmerized, I watch one that's closer
than the others, can almost feel
the energy propelling it through the air
and how every few seconds it harnesses
the huge wind. A flash of orange
and black and I gasp as, body streamlined now
like a plane's,
                    it nosedives into a savage sea
which is tossing up wave after wave.
At once its wings become flippers and, followed
by many others, it pursues a shoal of fish
darting into blue depths which soon darken.
I discover I'm in the waters too, glimpse
a fish being swallowed.
                    Seconds later
I'm swimming upwards. As soon as I reach
the ocean's surface I'm buffeted
by the salty air. Suddenly my arms open

46

and, as I rise, I pass gannets – masses of them,
covering a rocky island. When I reach the sky,
I look down and see everything is space,
everything is unfettered movement.

At Sunrise

After Annie Soudain

Because I can't see rolling hills
from my house, because I doubt that I'll ever

visit hills again, every day I look longingly
at the broad-backed Downs on the wall calendar

in my kitchen, longing to clasp the circle
of huge sun that's just risen behind them.

It's pale as a full moon and shedding
light on the gentle slopes and fields below.

Between the fields and a hedgerow
two trees have raised naked arms to the sky.

The sun appears to be resting
between them and the hedgerow seems

so near I feel I could touch the teasels –
their spiney heads are somehow satisfying

and they vie with fescue and parsley stalks
which lost their white flowerets months ago

but still hold out blackened spokes
tipped with dry seed heads. In our park

truculent brambles compete
with uncut grass but I long for a hedgerow

that's home to ragged robins, bugloss,
speedwell, wild roses. And now, in my head,

I'm walking among spring flowers.
Suddenly I see a long-legged hare

tearing over the fields and, easy
in my body again, I follow it towards the hills.

BREAKWATER

In memory of Elizabeth White, Historian. After Annie Soudain

The gaunt upright of the breakwater at the top
of the beach has been worn by centuries of tides
and winds. Above it, high in the sky, choughs

wheel among gannets and other high fliers.
Like them, these birds dive deep to snap up fish.
I was surprised to learn they're related to the rooks

which plague the trees in our park and quarrel
with flocks of seagulls on windy days in the winter.
Occasionally they even battle with a long-beaked heron

which suddenly flies up from the brook it inhabits,
flapping its wings. For a minute, I'm back in the past,
sitting by a half-buried breakwater on the beach

at West Wittering when I was eighteen, a raw girl
with my life before me. Now, I can't help wondering
if these Sussex breakwaters are also parts

of sacred circles like those on the Norfolk coast
and wondering too what circles meant
to the thinkers who lived many centuries ago.

CIRCLES

Midwinter and I'm lying on my bed making circles
with my legs. It's nearly midday, the sun is strong
but its warmth isn't touching our frostbound lawn.
Daydreaming, I picture the circle of Stonehenge
I saw on Face Book this morning: the ground
a black as thick as panther fur, spread out below
the dark sky and the sun a red globe that's resting
between two standing stones. For a moment
I glimpse my six-year-old son scrambling up
one of the massive blocks decades ago
when even cows were allowed to wander
anywhere in this place. Closing my eyes,
I try to visualize the series of wooden circles
scientists have discovered are lying beneath
the stone henges and for moments I conjure up
others on plateaus far beyond Wiltshire.
A phone ringing in the faraway hall pulls me
back to the present. Slowly, I come to, wander
downstairs and all day I feel in awe of the long-
ago thinkers who observed the circling of the sun
and worked out that its movements were key to everything.

The present Stonehenge was built on the site of earlier henges

2,500 years ago.

THREE

HILDEGARD

It's not the cold slithering like an endless worm
through her body that's making her shiver,
it's the startling white of the snow that's everywhere

and the yellow sun battering her head with light.
She grips mother's hand but keeps quiet
even though, now she's five, she has found

a secret word for *the thing*. She tries to forget her skin
feels too tight and to shut out the ringing
and ringing of the bells calling everyone to church.

The light dims as they enter the sacred building
but the windows let streams of it through
and the candles start flickering so madly that pain

strikes behind her eyes, becomes a blade
that slices her body in two. She holds her breath,
knowing it's happening again and that she can't stop it:

a strange visit from above which only she will receive.
Willing herself not to fall on the floor, she waits
until shining ropes raise her to the sky.

Now, she's not only standing by the priests
before the altar but also in a distant place with people
unknown to her, is certain God has brought her here.

When the place fades, she sways. They take her home
to bed, bring potions but she doesn't say
she's different from other children, not even to mother.

Fourteen years old, she has well-formed breasts,
knows why her body has monthly bleedings.
Since the age of six she's known she belongs to God

but she's had to wait all these years till today
to leave her family and be received into the monastery
at Disibodenberg. For hours she lies on the floor, her body

pressed against juniper branches. Its tart scent
stings her throat and her hand trembles when she stands
in the chancel holding the candles a priest has blessed.

How wildly their flames flicker as she places them
on the altar. Skeins of light dazzle her eyes
but she feels bereft when she's wrenched away from father,

sisters, brothers and her dearly beloved mother
but joy rises within her like beautiful waters
in a fountain as her worldly life slips away

and she is born into a spiritual life. In this God
will be her father and Jutta, who's been her guide
and teacher since she was eight, will be her spiritual mother.

In her new life Jutta teaches her Latin and how to play
the psaltery but she still yearns to learn more.
She loves the pattern of daily silences, the praying

and chanting which bring her closer to all-seeing God.
She loves too, the quiet which dwells in the monastery,
its dark walls, its solitude above the valley, the woods

whose trees travel to the sky as if on a pilgrimage
to heaven. She's elated when she breathes in
the nuttiness of damp leaves and strokes mosses

soft as rabbit fur. In spring she walks among windflowers
and carpets of blue bells, listens to warblers
whose notes blend with their own singing of psalms.

4

Four years to the day since she entered the monastery
but although she's been given the life she's always wanted,
she's troubled by Jutta's belief in the importance of fasting,

feels it's wrong to punish the body by withholding food.
That night she lies sleepless in bed, distressed
by Jutta's strictness and worried that visions come

to others in dreams and trances while her own
always occur in streams of strange light at times
when she's fully awake. Tossing and turning in bed,

it feels as though she's in a void. Tears fill her eyes
and she's overcome with a longing to see her mother,
to be enfolded in her arms, comforted by her voice.

She soothes herself by picturing the moon high
in the sky – she'd seen its unwavering silver beam
earlier, lighting up the path into the woods.

The next day, still in the grip of unhappiness,
she walks alone in the quiet woods and after a while
struggles up a steep path to a small cave

where she sits sobbing till a scent like the fragrance
of her mother's breath reaches her. In a broken voice
she asks: 'Where is your daughter now?

.

What will become of her?' Her tears don't stop
but the feeling of that dear presence is a comfort.
Rays of light fall between massive trunks

and she catches again the scent of her mother's breath –
it's as if hand in hand they're walking through a pool
of sun in a blue-belled garden of paradise.

5

Seven years later, when Jutta's piety and teachings
have brought more women to the monastery,
she tells her in private: 'The day will come when I will die,

then you must succeed me as abbess.' Yet she still
doubts her gifts, still yearns for more knowledge.
One morning she notices the trees are shedding

red and yellow leaves, a warning that winter
is hovering in the woods. When she opens the door
cold rushes at her, frost bites into her body

and she gasps when fiery flames suddenly descend
from the sky. The red tongues pierce her brain
but they don't burn. Instead, like kindness, they warm

her shivering flesh and suddenly she's aware
of understanding every word in the Bible,
even meanings of lines which she knows are beyond

her comprehension. Troubled, still questioning
the verity of her visions, she tells no one
about the disturbing visitation, stores it in herself.

6

Fifteen years later Jutta dies and it's unnerving
to find herself in charge of the large group of women.
She feels as though she's a tree in danger

of toppling into a fast-flowing river. Even so, she begins
to make changes: insists the eighteen sisters
serve God by eating well and taking care of their health.

She rules that in church they must wear white veils
with gold crowns to signify they are His virgins.
Fear of the power that's now hers continues

to plague her but she prays in her cell for guidance,
begs God to give her nights of peaceful sleep.
Then comes the day when hammers seem to strike

her head and her neck is tightly gripped. She hears
words coming from far above: 'Fragile human,
ashes of ashes, say and write what you see and hear.'

The command is repeated as if to make sure she obeys.
The sky opens, light pours, her body's released
and blood gushes through it like rain filling a river.

7

What a blessing it is when the day comes that Volmar,
the learned monk from whom she's learnt much
over many years, is allowed to be her helper,

her scribe in the mighty task of writing her book
which will set out the interpretations of heaven and earth
she's received from God. She confides in the monk

that her sleep is sometimes troubled by dreams
questioning her visions. Concerned, Volmar tells
the Abbot of her fears. He summons her at once

and standing tall above her, announces in a voice
ominous as thunder that her visions must be verified.
His eyes are fierce as a hawk's but she can tell he's afraid

of retaining her if she's a heretic even though
she's revered by the many who travel to the monastery
to seek her advice. For week after interminable week,

while the Pope's envoys stay in the Abbey
to observe and question, sharp pains pierce her limbs.
She can rarely attend to her visitors many of whom

look like terrified birds, can't explain why they've come,
and need her to see into their minds. Her strength
doesn't come back until she hears Pope Eugene

has praised and read passages from her *Scivias*
to prelates while at a synod in Trier. He also sends her
a letter in which praises her spiritual work.

8

More sisters come to the abbey and she worries
that the women now have little privacy for contemplation.
Often it bothers her too that there is no fit place

for all the visitors who come to seek her help. One day
she awakens to light and darkness clashing together
and hears God's powerful voice ordering her to move

her flock of women away from the dark monastery,
take them to a place by a river near Rupertsberg
and there erect a building on the site of a derelict abbey.

When her request is mocked by the monks and ignored
by Abbot Cuno she's seized by an illness which nails down
her limbs. Day after day she lies in bed, head aching,

eyes clouded. After a long time the Abbot visits
her cell and, shaken to see her lifeless as a pile of stones,
agrees to let her take her women elsewhere

and do what she wishes but he mutters that her plan
is foolish. At once energy surges through her body
and she springs up like a dog eager to chase a rabbit.

Alight with joy and triumph, she goes to the church,
glad of its huge candlelit silence, kneels in the calm
beneath the arches and windows. After a while

she steps outside into night's cool. High in the sky
the moon is a silver gladness. Its beam falls on the track
which leads into the woods where she still loves to walk

whenever she can. Aware of music playing in her head
and a peacefulness she's rarely known, she returns
to her cell and falls into a deep and dreamless sleep.

9

Re-settling her women is a long-drawn-out battle but one
she never wavers from even though they're forced to live
in what is little more than a ruin until she obtains ownership

of the site and building can begin. She immerses herself
in studying the essentials of construction and design
and when at last work starts, she oversees the labourers,

making sure they're kept separate from her flock. Month
after month they live in makeshift conditions and sometimes
visions of ladders climbing up to heaven surprise her.

Persuading Abbot Cuno, who's continued to berate
her stupidity, to release Volmar, her faithful scribe
and friend, is a different kind of battle but in the end

she wrenches him away by writing a furious letter
in the voice of God: 'I WHO AM say you are a robber
if you don't release this shepherd of spiritual medicine.'

10

At last, the magnificent abbey stands proud, a place
of comfort for her and her daughters and with space
for all the visitors. Some have bodily maladies,

some are troubled in their minds – always she eases
their sufferings. Often childless wives seek her out
and she instructs them on how to conceive a child.

Even scholarly priests come to consult her.
Senior prelates write for advice and every day
she interrupts her own writings to answer all her letters.

Everywhere she sees lapses among the clergy
and God sends her visions of the Church
as a lovely lady whose face and gown are besmirched.

He urges her to journey far and wide to preach
his word and though she is often so ill she is forced
to write her books and letters from her bed by whispering

to Volmar, who works seated at her side, she is given
the strength to rise up, travel to distant countries
and speak to huge crowds waiting to hear her words.

Years of writing and hard work pass and age
has furrowed her face when the clergy at Mainz send
a missive ordering her to stop celebrating mass at once

and disinter from their sacred grounds a man
who had cast off the church even though, later in life,
he'd returned to its fold. Furious and afraid,

she first calms her women, then trying to calm herself,
she writes to the archbishop saying that, terrified
by his command, she'd prayed for guidance

and immediately seen a vision of the calamity
which would overcome them all if the man is dug up
from the ground and moved. Seething, she adds

that she cannot disobey God. The archbishop
finally gives way but he sends a lengthy letter
chiding her. Enraged, she asks herself why a prelate

believes she should be answerable to him,
she who was chosen by God as a small child
and who has worked on his behalf for many decades.

12

The distressing day comes when Volmar,
her devoted helper and friend, her beloved son, dies.
That evening she sits in the silent church alone,

gazes at candle shadows licking the floors
and walls, thinks about his life and her own.
Most of all she's wanted to teach people about God

who created the world: the wonder of birds

singing in trees, swans floating whitely on rivers,
the fleet running of deer, the love humans

offer one another. She remembers the vision
she had of a precious child in the womb
and God's presence in the sky above as eyes

in a golden kite whose string trailed down
and became the umbilical cord delivering
the baby's soul. Her knees creak as she rises

from her seat and slowly makes her way outside.
The sky is alive with the shimmering dots of stars.
They beckon as if aware her earthly life is almost over.

See notes in Appendix

Artemesia Gentileschi

The anger has been building inside her for a long time –
maybe it began when she was seven and spent hours
staring at the paintings in the house, those which Father
brought home, his own and others by artists he worked with.
She longed to hold a brush and paint. If she was a boy

he would certainly have taken her to the studio
and she'd have learnt how to draw, how to map out.
By the time she became a woman and the blood she shed
each month was brighter than the skin of a ripe
red apple she was all too aware that women were treated

as mindless: playthings, babymakers, slaves, nothings,
and her anger was as hard as nutshells. At last though,
Father started taking her to the busy studio and training
her to be an artist. Excitement rushed through her
the morning she first used golds, pinks and sky-blue

on canvas and each night when she lay down to sleep
studies of figures and colours danced inside her head.
She felt inspired by the paintings of the great Caravaggio
and determined to create work that matched his. By the time
she was seventeen her skills far outstripped her brothers'.

It was then that her father brought Signor Tasso to their house
as her tutor. She was shocked – how he could be blind
to the character of this so-called artist? His work was inferior
to Caravaggio's and he was known to be a rogue, a lecher.
How was it Father failed to see this person of ill-repute

would cause havoc in their household? Worse, he seemed
to be considering the unsavoury man as a suitor.
She wasn't surprised when this *tutor* showed little interest
in teaching and instead kept staring greedily at her breasts
as if he couldn't wait to push her down and grab them.

His smile taunted, seemed to dare her to resist his advances.
On his third visit he suddenly started to claw at her clothing.
She tried to kick him, scratch his face with her fingernails,
bite his hands but he shook her as if she was a cushion.
Then, swearing like a devil he tore the bodice of her gown.

She screamed and screamed for Tuzia, the woman
who was supposed to chaperone her, but she didn't appear
although she must have heard. No doubt he had bribed
and bedded this servant just as he bedded others.
All she could do was spit at her aggressor and try to kick him.

Uttering obscenities no woman should hear, he flung her
on a couch, ripped half her clothes off and, unbothered
that she was a virgin, raped her. It took her days
to make Father believe the truth about her attacker
but in the end she showed him her torn and stained gown.

Furious, he proclaimed the man must marry her, ignored
her cries of revulsion. She uttered prayers of thanks
that the evil creature showed no sign of interest
in making her his wife – he was probably busy raping
other women. Understanding finally, the kind of villain

he was dealing with, Father pressed charges. A date
was fixed for the trial but this didn't make her life any better.
The whole of Rome muttered about her. In the court
everyone gawped and the sessions went on and on
through the sizzling heat of summer when the city's streets

stank of rotten vegetables and mangy dogs yapped
at heels. Each day more people tried to squeeze inside
to see the drama and if they couldn't squash into the room
they made a racket in the street. Tasso was accused
of many crimes yet it was as if *she* was the main criminal.

With thick cords they tied up her hands – the hands
she needed to paint – then the ropes were pulled so tight
they cut through her skin, almost broke her finger bones.
The pain was terrible. This torture was meant to force her
to tell the truth – as if she hadn't already! She'd done nothing

to deserve such treatment. In the end the case was won
but now she's fuming because the sentence against Tasso,
exiling him from Rome, hasn't been carried out. Weeks
it's taken for her fingers to heal but she's almost ready
to start work again and release the fury boiling inside her

in the painting she's been planning. It will show the world
the debauched face of Holofernes, the general who was greedy
to strip the beautiful maiden Judith of every garment
she was wearing, his delight that he's lured her, a girl
who appeared to be lost, into his tent. She'll depict herself

plying him with wine until he lies in a stupor on his bed,
herself clad in a stormy blue gown standing by her maid,
both of them holding him down. The light will fall
on his arms as he struggles to fight off his assailants
and on the arms of the two women straining to keep him still.

Their stance will show the effort needed to raise the sword
and start hacking the head. She knows the finished work
will be her first masterpiece, believes in time she'll become
as famous as Caravaggio, be remembered for her paintings
of women as artists, goddesses, mothers nursing their babies.

FOUR

Five Views of Mount Fuji

For John K. After Hokusai

A Shower below the Summit

Don't linger by the cherry blossom in the valley
even if you're feeling fragile, a voice insists
in my head*, when you begin to climb*

the mountain will be irresistible. Maybe I should –
I'd gaze at the dramatic deepening of pinks
on its sides to reds and a moody plum-black,

gasp at that surprising skitter of lightning
and the strange hieroglyphics it writes
on the lower slopes to show this ground

is sacred. Already I can see myself higher
than the birches and beeches, the firs longing
to scramble to the summit, above the treeline.

Imagine looking down on those docile hills,
feeling close to that flock of clouds, cupping
hands to catch their swirling feathers, delighting

in a sky which heralds hope with its hint of coral,
in the blessing of snow on the volcano's crest
and the trickles from it, gentle as slumber.

Once I'm standing on the summit I'll forget
the worrying world below. Fuji, keeper
of the secret of immortality, will enfold me.

River

Down here on the plain the river flows
with such confidence. Its banks and bushes
sing with green, and the bridge spanning it

with a single arch is so graceful it makes
my heart leap. Intriguing, the stream of people
with parasols eager to cross. Some stop

to watch the men in the rowing boats
who are preoccupied with persuading fish
to bite. The unmanned craft visible

through the tall piers and idling on the waters,
look like benign creatures basking.
In the distance, unmistakeable, is stalwart Fuji.

And what I shall never forget is how
in the small hours this morning when I lost
my footing, slipped into bottomless marsh

and was struggling against the black liquid
sucking me in, I was suddenly aware of the river,
and how I summoned the strength to pull free

as soon as I saw Fuji across the plain,
its peak white-headed, a beacon of hope
which anyone can view from anywhere.

Measuring the Pine Tree

At the Mishima Pass, close to Fuji now,
I shed my backpack and, like the other pilgrims,
I stare at the pine tree. Even the lowest

of the straight-backed trunk's branches
seem to brush the sky. It is hard to believe
it's only an illusion that it's soaring

to heaven, an illusion that it's outstripped
great Fuji which is rising serenely
behind it. The trail of white cloud emerging

from the peak has almost shaped itself
into a dragon. Standing on humpy ground
heaped with snow, I become one of the three

trying to measure the tree's massive girth
by stretching arms right round the bole.
Not a chance, our six outspread limbs

can only span a fraction of the circumference.
We all laugh but in our hearts we know
we're no more than dots beside Fuji,

less if we consider the pinpricks of light
visible in the night sky, messages
sent from worlds in measureless space.

Blue Fuji

Morning and the misty layers are rising
to reveal Fuji is in a blue mood, not the blue
of melancholy music, not the blue of depression,

no, Fuji is wearing blues that are alert yet calming:
benign azures sift into lapis lazulis which promise
cloudless midnights and below, turquoise

has capped the foothills. The sea's in pale attire
and hankering for the sky but its inlets are seeking
ultramarines. I love it that the waters and hills

have found easy undulations – not a straight line
to be seen. Even the peak of mighty Fuji
is a squiggle not a point. As for the cranes,

the enchanting cranes, which flew through
my room as I drifted into sleep last night,
they stand on jointed stalks that end in splayed toes,

their backs curved like ballet dancers',
their necks long and sinuous. Two seem
to be engaged in badinage as they preen and feed.

Another pair of these couriers of longevity
are skimming the sky, necks outstretched, wings
purposeful, as they head towards Mount Fuji.

The Great Wave

Magnificent as an emperor the wave rears up
and I gasp at the height, the extravagance
of its royal blue and foaming white, the roar

which outdoes a lion as it shapes a dragon
spewing spume far into the sky
to proclaim its success in dwarfing sacred Fuji,

its determination to dominate the world
once it's devoured the many-headed worms
slithering between the lower snowy peaks.

But the truth is the heads belong to fishermen
who have the skill to navigate their boats
through clefts in the tumultuous waters

and are joking as they race one another
to the shore to start selling the day's catch.
The wave is huge but to mighty Fuji,

which in the distance appears tiny, it's less
than a grasshopper, a raindrop, a speckle.
I relax and wait for the immense crest,

all the pomp and circumstance it carries,
to collapse, aware that Fuji who has overseen
humankind for millennia, Fuji will endure.

Katsushika Hokusai (1760-1849) was a Japanese printmaker of the Edo period.
The sequence is inspired by prints in the series Thirty-six Views of Mount Fuji.

Acknowledgements

Credit is due to the following magazines where some of these poems, or earlier versions of them, first appeared:

Acumen, ARTEMIS poetry, Dreamcatcher, Frogmore Papers, The High Window online magazine, The London Grip online magazine, Pennine Platform, Poetry & All that Jazz, Raceme, Stand.

Five Views of Mount Fuji was first published as a booklet in which each poem was accompanied by a reproduction of the print it related to. (Fisherrow 2017, Editor: John Killick).
The Word was highly commended in the Binstead Poetry Competition in 2021 and published in *Poetry & All that Jazz* in 2021.
Fishing Boats was shortlisted for the Frogmore Papers Poetry Prize in 2022 and published in the special 40th anniversary issue in spring 2023.
The Glory was shortlisted in the Second Light Competition in 2022.

I want to express my gratitude to my husband, Erwin Schneider, for the huge amount of support and help he gives me which enables me to have space and time for writing poetry.

I am indebted to Dilys Wood for her continuing encouragement and belief in my work, for looking carefully at the two long poems in this book and in particular for helping me work out the best way to arrange the poems for this collection. In addition, I want to thank her and Anne Stewart for bringing out my collection *Siege and Symphony* under the Second Light Publications imprint in 2021.

I am also indebted to Caroline Price for her in-depth feedback on almost all the poems in this book, also her friendship and her support of my work for over thirty years.

I want to express gratitude to Mimi Khalvati, friend of many years, for her belief in my work, the example of her own outstanding poetry and for the kind and thoughtful support she's given me in the last few years.

A special thank-you is due to John Killick who first saw the possibilities of my work and published my debut collection in 1984 and the next four books until he ceased to run Littlewood Press, also for his friendship over many years and feedback on many of my poems.

Special thanks is also due to Stephen Stuart-Smith, Director of Enitharrmon and Isabel Brittain, his right hand, for taking my work on in the 1990s and publishing my poetry until 2014 when lack of funding from the Arts Council forced him to stop producing poetry collections.

Thanks is due too to Adele Ward of Ward Wood Publishing for bringing out my collection *Lifting the Sky* in 2018.

I also want to express gratitude to Simon Richey for his poetry and for poetry conversations on the phone and here at my house since the summer of the pandemic.

I am indebted to Robert Aldous and Chris Holley for their paintings and collaborations over the last few years. They have both inspired poems in this book. These are separately acknowledged.

I'm also very grateful to Sue Sims for bringing out this collection, to Robert Aldous for allowing his painting, *San Vito lo Capo*, to be used as the image for the front cover and to Martin Parker for designing the cover of the book.

Previous Titles

Poetry

Fistful of Yellow Hope, Littlewood Press 1984
Cat Therapy, Littlewood Press 1986
Cathedral of Birds, Littlewood Press 1988
Crossing Point, Littlewood Press 1991,
Exits, Enitharmon 1994
The Panic Bird, 1998
Insisting on Yellow: New & Selected Poems, Enitharmon 2000
Multiplying the Moon, Enitharmon 2004
Circling the Core, Enitharmon 2008
What Women Want (pamphlet) Second Light Publications 2012
The Door to Colour Enitharmon 2014
Persephone in Finsbury Park (pamphlet) Second Light Publications 2016
Lifting the Sky, Ward Wood Publishing 2018
Siege and Symphony Second Light Publications 2021

Prose

Marigold's Monster, Heinemann 1976
If Only I Could Walk Heinemann 1977
Will the Real Pete Roberts Stand Up 1978
Writing for Self-Discovery, with John Killick, Element Books 1998
Writing My Way Through Cancer, Jessica Kingsley 2003
Writing Your Self, with John Killick, Continuum International 2009

Poetry Anthologies, as co-editor:

Parents, Enitharmon 2000
Making Worlds, Headland 2003
Four Caves of the Heart, Second Light Publications
Images of Women, Arrowhead Press 2006
Her Wings of Glass, Second Light Publications 2014

Appendix

p.52 **HILDEGARD**

The main source for this poem was *Hildegard of Bingen*, an in-depth biography by Fiona Maddocks *faber and faber* (2013). Hildegard was born in 1098 and died in 1179. She was both a visionary and a genius with a considerable knowledge of many subjects. She composed music which was noted down. This was re-discovered towards the end of the twentieth century and it is still played today. Learned in medicine, she acted as a doctor. She wrote several books and was a significant figure in mediaeval Europe. In my poem I have traced her life with a focus on her visions. In describing these I have drawn directly from Hildegard's own accounts, which are quoted often at length, in the biography by Fiona Maddocks. I also drew on other twelfth century writings about Hildegard which are quoted from and discussed in Fiona Maddocks' text. Her book includes colour photographs of some of the images recording Hildegard's extraordinary visions. I studied these images and others reproduced on the internet. The visions must have been recorded as paintings either by Hildegard herself or by someone who reproduced them as she instructed.